HEALTH AND EXERCISE

HEALTH AND EXERCISE

Edited & Compiled by

Dr. A.K. Srivastava

M.P.Ed., N.I.S. (Athletics), D.Y. Ed., Ph.D. (Phy. Edu.)
Director, Physical Education
Delhi Engineering College, Bawana Road, Delhi-110042

SPORTS PUBLICATION

7/26, Ground Floor, Ansari Road,
Darya Ganj, New Delhi-110002
Phones: (Office) 65749511 (Fax) 011-23240261
(Mobile) 9868028838 (Residence) 27562163
E-mail: lakshaythani@hotmail.com

Published by:

SPORTS PUBLICATION
7/26, Ground Floor, Ansari Road, Darya Ganj, New Delhi-110002
Ph. : (Office) 65749511, 23240261 (Mobile) 9868028838
         (Residence) 27562163 (Fax) 011-23240261
E-mail: *lakshaythani@hotmail.com*

© 2010 Publishers

I.S.B.N: 978-81-7879-582-9

PRINTED IN INDIA 2010

Laser Typeset by:
JAIN MEDIA GRAPHICS,
C-4/95-A, Keshav Puram, Delhi-35

Printed by:
Vishal Kaushik Printers
A-49, Gali No. 6, Jagat Puri Extn.,
Delhi-110093

Price: Rs. 195/-

CONTENTS

1

ARE YOU DOING THE RIGHT EXERCISE

Did you know there are different workouts devoted to different age groups? If at 50s, you do exercises meant for a 30 years-old, you could be in trouble.

Crash diets. Late nights. Sporadic exercises. Fast food......... Modern living offers many permutations in our zeal to enjoy life while trying to be fit too. Recent international studies reveal how crash diet actually adds up to your girth and thereby woes. It is important to eat healthy food regularly in small quantities and drinks lots of fluid, and at the same time reduce your alcohol and caffeine intake.

"Bones stop growing after 18 years, but muscles grow till you die. They burn calories even when you are at rest." So, well-tones muscles can keep you trim and healthy. They protect your joints, prevent arthritis and spondylitis, and there's even a lesser chance of ligament damage in case of minor injury. Just regular pull-up, push-ups and swimming with some light-weight training can do wonders. And yes, irrespective of age, some exercise is a must. Warm-ups and stretches are a necessity before you start and cool down do sometime after the exercise.

There needs to be a certain discipline and relaxation in your daily schedule. For example, relaxation techniques like Shavasana daily for 20 minutes (research shows it helps regulate blood pressure better than drugs!). Similarly, never allow your breath, heartbeat or pulse rate (when not exercising) to become fast as it corrodes your lifespan. In that case, simply start watching your breath and it will gradually slow down. Practice silence daily starting from 5 minutes, increasing up to 30 minutes everyday. Some easy exercises for various ages to live longer.

1.1 20-30 YEARS

Fitness mantra: If you feel acidity on most days, reorganize your eating habits.

Must do: Can opt for a melange of vigorous activities like outdoor running; group games like volleyball; or an individual sport like tennis or squash.

Better avoid: Don't overdo any activity. Avoid playing when injured.

Guru mantra: Treat one day in a week as the rest day.

1.2 30-40 YEARS

Fitness Mantra: You start panting after climbing stairs, start exercising regularly and check the number of breaths per minute.

Must do: Enroll in an organized fitness program. Start weight training (especially females) to arrest loss of bone density, or join any vigorous dance class. For both genders, calcium intake is important. Women should go for regular checkups for breast cancer. As the aging process has set in, start yoga or any other stretching exercises to combat it. When working on the PC monitor or watching television, do not forget to blink.

Better Avoid: Don't just workout on weekends only.

Guru Mantra: Go for an eye check-ups and get lipid profile (a group of blood tests that gives the pattern of fat in an individual to determine the risk of coronary heart diseases) and blood sugar tests done.

1.3   40-50 YEARS

Fitness Mantra: If you are tired on walking up, count your heart rate daily and check blood pressure regularly.

Must do: Switch towards less vigorous exercises like golf and brisk walking. Start learning music– because it will stimulate activity in dormant brain cells, which can slow down the aging process. Learn water sport or swimming (for females it lowers hot flushes during meopause and for men it improves fat loss).

Better Avoid: This is favourite time for diseases like diabetes and hypertensions. So start cubing on your salt and sugar intake.

Guru Mantra; To prevent wrinkles, fill

your mouth with water and count up to five and then spit it out. It cleans the oral cavity and increases blood circulation on the face and tones facial muscles. Visit a doctor for a thorough clinical test and go for regular eye check-ups.

1.4 50-60 YEARS

Fitness Mantra: If you tend to forget easily, enroll in a yoga class and do something adventurous 2-3 times a year.

Must do: With age, digestion capacity of the body declines sharply maintain oral hygiene as it plays a significant role in prevention of urine infections. Diabetes and heart diseases. Brisk walk, golf and swimming should be your exercises intinerary. Men should go for regular prostrate cancer check-ups.

Better Avoid: This is the age where osteoarthritis of knees can occur. If the knees are painful, treadmill should be avoided and low impact exercise like, cycling should be adopted.

Guru Mantra: Go for adventure sports

(river rafting/outdoor camp) or yoga holiday.

1.5   60 YEARS AND ABOVE

Fitness Mantra: If you feel less energetic on most days. Learn meditation and have realistic expectations from people around you!

Must do: To avoid Alzheimer's disease, start ,mental exercise like Sodoku. Golf, simple stretches, walking and regular massages are recommended. Swimming, being part of laughter groups and yoga holidays with like-minded people will be a cure to loneliness. Also, get involved with some social welfare activities.

Better avoid: Don't do any activity that could precipitate or worsen knee and back problems.

Guru Mantra: Lie down on the bed and lift hips, but use 2-3 pillows to support them. Rest your hips, legs and feet against the wall, back resting on the bed and stay that way for 15 minutes. Practice this twice daily as it prevents swelling in the feet and gives relief to varicose veins and improves blood circulation.

2

SOME EASY FITNESS TESTS TO BE DONE ONCE IN EVERY SIX WEEKS

2.1 Pinch the fat around your waist between thumb and index finger, if the fat volume is more than an inch, it is bad news.

2.2 Sit on the ground with legs straight, bend forward and touch the toes without lifting the knee. Your flexibility will hint at your fitness.

2.3 Count how many sit-ups (abdominal strength) and push-ups (not necessarily to be done at one go) without much discomfort, you are not bad. It is over 30, it is excellent.

2.4 The three-minute step test is a simple measurement of endurance. All you need is a sturdy stool or a bench that's 20 cms high and a watch. This idea is to step up and down on it for three minutes. The rate of stepping is important. You need to climb up and down 24 times a minute or twice in five seconds. Put your right foot up and then the left, and put them down in the same order. A steady rhythm is maintained between the four steps. After three minutes of continuous stepping up and down, rest for 30 seconds. Then, count your pulse for another 30 seconds and then multiply it by two. That will give you the pulse rate per minutes. Now refer to the table to know how you have fared.

2.4.1 PULSE RATE (PER MINUTE) AT 30 SECONDS-MEN

AGE	EXCELLENT	GOOD	FAIR	POOR
20-30	74	76-84	86-100	>102
30-40	78	80-86	88-100	>102
40-50	80	82-88	90-104	>106
50+	83	84-90	92-104	>106

2.4.2 PULSE RATE (PER MINUTE) AT 30 SECONDS-WOMEN

AGE	EXCELLENT	GOOD	FAIR	POOR
20-30	86	88-92	93-110	>112
30-40	86	88-94	95-112	>114
40-50	88	90-94	96-114	>116
50+	90	92-98	100-116	>118

The step test tells you how well your cardiovascular system responds to exercise and how quickly it recovers. Periodic testing is recommended with other tests.

3

HOW TO EXERCISE
A STIFF NECK?

3.1 Many people suffer from neck stiffness and soreness. When you sit throughout the day, tension can build up; muscles become tight. It's a good idea to stretch periodically, and to 'exercise' your neck.

3.2 The neck push; This can be done sitting or standing and helps strengthen your neck muscles. Keeping your head upright, hold the palm of the one hand against your forehead, and press your head forward. Resisting with your palm. Hold for 10 to 15 seconds. Now clasp your hands behind your head, and press your head backward, resisting with your hands. Hold for 10 to 15 seconds.

3.3 Now hold your right hands against the side of your head, and press your head to the right, resisting with your hand. Hold for 10 to 15 seconds, repeat on left side.

3.4 Relax and roll your head in a circular motion.

3.5 For tense, aching neck; Relax your shoulders and let your head roll forward, chin to chest. Slowly rotate your head in a circle without straining your neck. Repeat five times. Relax. Then rotate in the opposite direction and repeat five times. Try not to raise your shoulders as you do this exercise.

4

BACKBONE OF HEALTH

4.1 After warm-up and strengthening asanas for the back, we now move on to toning and stretching. The asanas too should be performed in this order; at your pace, and level of flexibility.

4.2 For toning, lie on your stomach with hands interlocked behind your neck and legs straight. Inhale and raise your upper body as high as you can. Exhale and lower your body to the ground. Do 10 to 15 rounds.

4.3 VIPRIT NAUKASANA (INVERTED BOAT POSE)

4.3.1 Lie on your stomach with legs together and arms stretched above your head.

4.3.2 Exhale and lift your arms and legs up as high as possible and hold this position for a few seconds and then lower them.

4.3.3 Repeat five to six rounds.

The next two exercises are for stretching the back.

4.4 PAWANMUKTASANA

4.4.1 Lie flat on back with hands by the side of your thighs.

4.4.2 Interlock your fingers, bend right knees, place your hands over your knee and slowly exhale and pull your knee towards your chest.

4.4.3 Raise upper body and bring chin over your knees.

4.4.4 Hold this posture for 30 seconds to a minute and breathe normally.

4.4.5 Relax your grip, straighten your leg and come back to original position.

4.4.6 Repeat with other leg (these two steps are Ek pad pawanmusktasana) and then with both legs pressed towards your chest (poorna pawanmuktasana).

4.5 SHARNAGAT MUDRA

4.5.1 Stand on your knees and then sit on your heels with toes touching each other.

4.5.2 Stretch your arms above your head.

4.5.3 Keep your ears between your arms and stretch forward. Try to keep your bottom on the heels.

4.5.4 With your bottom touching your heels, bend forward and place your arms on the floor in front of you, with your forehead touching the floor.

4.5.5 Breathe normally as you hold this position as long as you are comfortable.

5

STAY HYDRATED,
STAY HEALTHY

It is essential that you keep yourself well hydrated while exercising, so that your skin retains its glow, and you don't feel drained and exercise lagged! And no, lugging a bottle isn't the only way to stay hydrated during your workout..........

So, if you hate holding a water bottle while you walk, then think of other ways. Because, hydration is essential when you are exercising. How much you need and when you need it really depends on the length of your walk and the intensity of your walk. A casual stroll while chatting with a friend is a very different half hour spent than a fast, high intensity walk.

The general rule to thumb, however, is a woman of average weight needs about half a litre of water for every 15 minutes of exercise for longer than 90 minutes, consider having a sports drink after your workout to replenish your body with the nutrients and elextrolytes it needs. Just remember, sports drinks are full of sugar and are unnecessary calories for regular workouts. So use them just for those 'in training' periods, when doing long workouts preparing for an event. For example, drink after two-hours of gymming or dance practices. If carrying a water bottle as you exercise is problematic for you, try these different options.

There are now waist packs that hold a water bottle, as well as your car keys and or a cell phone. This will free up your hands while you are walking. Freeze your water bottle for hot days and as it melts it stays cold for a longer period of time– it will also you're your lower back cool.

Try out a hydration system. You can find them at most sports stores. It offers a constant stream of water as you are moving. This is a great option of longer walks and can be used even while skiing or on long bike rides.

Set up your walks and runs on paths where you know there are drinking fountains nearby– like jogger's tracks in parks.

6

SOME SIMPLE WAYS
TO STAY FIT

Exercise is never a waste of time; it's an important part of a healthy lifestyle. It reduces your risk of heart attack and is an essential component in controlling body weight.

It's also something you can do with other people, which can be great fun. So, there's no time like the present to make that commitment to yourself to find time to exercise and improve your health. There are many simple ways to stay active and healthy. Plan your week so you have to walk to the shops frequently. By going often you'll only have to carry light bags of shopping back.

Looking at ways, in which you can be more active in and around your home, this will do wonders to your body. Use the stairs to exercise, work on the garden or install some gym equipment. Simple activities like vacuuming, cleaning or arranging your bookshelves are ways to keep your body moving.

Participating in community-based activity programmes in your local area, will help you unwind and relax. Joining fitness classes is not always the only way to stay fit, just anything that gets you moving is as good as joining a gym. Conservation groups can be a great way to get involved in improving your local environment and being active at the same time.

7

TUMMY TUCKERS

7.1 GOOD CUPPA

It's what beautiful damsels on the catwalk drink for a flat stomach. Sip dandelion tea a few times in the day. Dandelion's bitter compounds reduce water retention and spruce up digestion. It also acts as a mild locative, helping you to clean your system effectively.

7.2 BALL GAME

Sitting on an exercise ball is one of the easiest ways to tone your abs. You could do this at your desk, or while watching television. Do it for a fortnight and you will definitely see taut abs peeping out of your tee! You could go ahead and do sets of crunches, but make sure that you balance yourself well before you start off. An instructor at hand is recommended.

7.3 WAIST DEEP

Tie a string around your waist, so that every time your slouch or slacken your abdominal muscles, it will pinch, making you sit up! A favourite tip amongst trainers, this makes your muscles sweat, without trying too hard.

7.4 TAKE THE STAIRS

Next time you head towards the lift, turn back and take the good old stairs. Climbing makes your stomach muscles work harder. The result, a tauter tummy that makes you look leaner.

7.5 YOGA TO THE RESCUE

Experts recommend yoga as a great way to cut flab around the tummy. Additionally, it also gives you a good posture. It's a double deal hard to miss ladies!

8

WALKING MEDITATION

If you don't find the sitting posture appealing enough and like movement, walking meditation is a powerful alternative.

Walking meditation is probably as old as the first time we ever walked on our own, when we were naturally in the 'present'. On growing up too, we at times get our best ideas while walking! Meditation makes your walking a beautiful and peaceful experience. Here's how: Meditation in walking is a process of 'walking mindfully'. In this, we should always be in the moment and experience our walking with full awareness, paying full attention to mind-body races, we should not follow it. Simply watch your mind, your thoughts, without letting them involve you. Similarly, be aware of the physical movements. If your awareness strays with your mind, bring it back to your surroundings. Observe how your body, breathing, the air, your body, breathing, the air, feels. Every mindful step taken in meditation with greater self-awareness, fades stressful thoughts of the past and future, bringing you into the 'now'.

As we begin to discover the joy of walking in the 'present', we start developing the qualities of nature itself, such as peace, softness, calmness, gentleness, humidity, gratitude and clarity. Walking meditation enhances the vibrations under our feet, spreading these positive energies over the earth, that not only refreshes our mind-body but transforms our surroundings too. Remember, we are our true destination. If we walk on life's journey mindfully, we will know definitely and exactly what path we are on.

You may begin with walking in the 'now' for 15 minutes and gradually increase it to an hour daily. Walking alone is better as walking in a group may distract. But walking in a group can be wonderful if everyone chooses to retain their individual meditative states. This meditation should be for the sake of walking and not to 'get anywhere'. Even if you have a destination, do of let it concern you, so that only walking remains!

9

HOW BACKACHE CAN BE PREVENTED?

The following arsenal to combat backache.

9.1 FOOD FOR THOUGHT

9.1.1   Phosphorus improves bone mass density. It is found in raw egg yolk, whole barley, whole wheat, corn, lobsters, mushroom, raisins, milk, pumpkin, squash, garlic, massor dal, carrots, coriander, coconut, sesame seeds.

9.1.2   Calcium, which builds bones, is found in shrimps, apricots, figs, cabbage, celery, cauliflower, spinach, beetroot, raw onions, berries, radishes, dates, beans, curry leaves, parsley, soya beans, coriander.

9.1.3   Fluorine is good for strengthening bones and is found in goat milk, egg yolk, cabbage, cauliflower, brussels sprout, seafish, cheese, tomato, avocado.

9.1.4   Vitamin D helps build bones and is found in green vegetables, sunshine and cold-liver oil.

9.2   MASSAGE THOSE MUSCLES

9.2.1   Fat reduction and increases in muscles tone are essential. These can be achieved with yoga, pranayama and lightweight gym workout and walking.

9.2.2   You have to be extra careful while doing exercises. Always start with a five-minutes warm-up before the exercise and a cool down session after the exercise. Sudden, jerky movements can result in severe backache.

9.2.3   Therapeutic massage on tight areas and nodules of the back will help release fresh flow of bloo

10

PLAN YOUR POSTURE

The flexibility of the neck and back curves has to be maintained by relaxed good postural alignment. For example, sitting in a hunched manner is bad for the back. Never bend forward when you have a back problem. Standing for long hours is equally bad.

10.1 TO HELL WITH HEELS

High heels strain lower back. Hence, it is better to avoid wearing it.

10.2 SLIM YOUR HIPS

Here are some more yogic exercises that will help you shed flab around the hips. You need to be focussed and practise these exercises on a regular basis to get the desired results.

10.2.1 EXERCISE-A

- Stand straight. Spread your feet

apart and bring them parallel to your shoulders.

- Bend knees as much as possible and raise hands over your head.

- Exhale slowly, bend and place your palms on the floor, concentrate on the gap between your palms. Hold for as long as you can.

- Rise slowly you need to do this only once.

BENEFITS:

- Stretches hips muscles and removes extra flab on the hip.

- Strengthens knee-joint.

- Stretches the entire back.

Precautions : People suffering from severe knee pain or back problems should avoid this.

10.2.2 EXERCISE-B

- Lie on your right side and bend the right arm.

- Raise torso and head, supporting them on the right elbow, which remains on the floor.

- Rest the head on right palm.

- Place the left palm on the left thigh.

- Inhale and raise left leg as high as possible and grasp the big toe with your left hand. If this is too difficult, hold the leg as close to the foot as possible.

- Keep legs straight and hold your breath.

- While exhaling, lower the raised leg and arm to the starting position.

- Practice up to 10 times.

- Repeat on the other side.

BENEFITS:

- Reduces weight on the hips and thighs.

- Stretches the muscles of the

sides of the body, rendering them stronger and more flexible.

Precautions: People suffering from slopped disc, sciatica or cervical spondylitis should avoid this asana.

11

PILATES FOR
ABS AND BACK

Pilates is highly recommended for strengthening the back and spine. Three classes a week will result in increased mobility of joints, more toned thighs and waist, a flatter stomach and improved blood circulation.

All you need is a mat or a towel to get started. People of all age groups and fitness levels can do these exercises. It is great for

11.1 Overweight individuals and elderly since no lifting or jumping is involved.

11.2 Individuals suffering from arthritis because it helps reduce muscle stiffness.

11.3 Women who have just given birth and want to regain their body shape.

12

SPINAL MOBILITY

12.1 Lie on your back on mat, with you knees bent, heels opposite your sitting bones and hands resting on your lower abdomen with your arms relaxed. Inhale laterally and begins to draw your abdominal inwards.

12.2 Exhale, drawing your lower abdominal, inward, to initiate a pelvic tilt backward, stretching your lower back, and raise your hips off the floor. Make sure your buttocks are relaxed and your feet are firmly planted on the floor.

12.3 Inhale to roll your pelvis back to neutral, and relax your hips completely.

12.4 Repeat four to five times.

13

SKIPPING YOUR WAY
TO FITNESS

A rope screams through the air, energy is burnt with a sagging rate of 1,300 calories an hour, and a miracle of physical activity is performed. We're talking about skipping, an activity which is considered both fun as well as extremely healthy.

Despite many considering it time-consuming, skipping is fast making a comeback. And what's helping matters is the fact that it is not just an effective route to fitness but is a cost-and-time-saving exercise. For, as we've said before, it does not entail any of those heavy charges at the gym.

Young people are constantly amazed at what is possible with just a jumble, simple rope. Skipping four to five times a week, from a few minutes to a couple of hours a day not only helps you burn the extra flab' but is also beneficial for the cardio-vascular system.

And this is the key. Basic skipping is simple, and almost anyone who has five square feet of free space can easily do it. Skipping for about 10 minutes is said to be the equivalent of 30 minutes of jogging, as it tones the upper body as well as the legs.

Despite losing its appeal for quite sometime, for many men considered it an effective activity, skipping is back in favour now. Especially with boxers who rely on skipping for endurance training. So, next time you see a rope just do not hesitate to skip your flab away. It is healthy as well as an inexpensive habit.

14

DO'S AND DON'TS
OF WALKING

Walking is increasingly being rated as an excellent means of staying fit and healthy. It is a natural form of exercise that we do every day to some extent.

For those who consider it a form of exercise the risks of suffering an injury are low as long as you fallow a gradual programme and don't do too much too soon. All you need is a pair of comfortable shoes with adequate support and shock absorption and a watch with a second hand if you want to measure the intensity of your walk by measuring your heart rate. The benefits that you derive from walking are dependant on many factors that include, how frequently you walk, the distance covered and the intensity of your walks.

While a half-hour amble through the park might do wonders to reduce your stress levels, it would not do much in terms of weight loss too. However, a programme of regular brisk walking (six to eight km), combined with an energy-controlled, low-fat, high-carbohydrate diet should cut some body fat.

14.1 DO'S

14.1.1 Make your walks a priority. Unless you recognise them as an essential feature of your lifestyle, you will soon abandon them.

14.1.2 Try to convince a friend to join you. You can motivate one another and chat while walking. Ideally, get your spouse to walk too.

14.1.3 Invest in a good pair of walking shoes. Take the advice of well-trained staff at the shoe shop.

14.1.4 Set yourself a goal and reward yourself when you achieve it.

Positive reinforcement is strongly linked to success and sustainability.

14.1.5 Monitor your progress, keep track of the distance walked how long it took and what your exercising heart rate over a 10-second period is. Also measure your waist, hips and chest every month.

14.1.6 Find an attractive variety of routes to avoid boredom. A good idea is to measure out a 3-5 km route, which you walk as fast as you can once a week.

14.1.7 Read up on the benefits of regular walking, i.e. a decrease in your risk of suffering from heart disease, high blood pressure, high cholesterol, osteoporosis, osteoarthritis, obesity, type 2 diabetes, anxiety and depression. This information will strengthen your resolve.

14.2 DON'TS

14.2.1   Don't expect significant weight loss in the first few weeks. Walking 3-4 times a week at a moderate to high intensity can result in fat loss, if combined with high carbohydrate, low-fat meals.

14.2.2   Don't walk alone in the dark and wear a reflective belt/clothing at dawn or dusk.

14.2.3   Don't miss sessions early on in your programme. In a few months, you will probably be addicted to it.

14.2.4   Don't overdo it. Many people start off totally fired up and think that more is better and add in extra sessions. This leads to burn-out and is not sustainable.

14.3   **THE STARTING POINT**

14.3.1   Men over 40, women over the 50s and those with either a chronic disease or risk factors must seek medical advice.

14.3.2 Purchase a pair of suitable walking shoes, a watch with a second hand and a reflective belt.

14.3.3 Measure out routes ranging from 2-5 kms in a safe and attractive suburb.

14.3.4 Do some baseline measurements so that you have a point of reference to indicate progress.

14.3.5 Purchase some form of log book to record these measurements as well as your walking sessions.

14.3.6 Warm up for five minutes before starting out on your walk.

15

THINGS TO KEEP IN MIND WHILE DOING ABS EXERCISES

15.1 Although abdominal work is strenuous, it is imperative that you breathe properly while exercising. Exhale during the contraction of the muscle. Every time you tighten up, breathe out. Release all your breath, even when working the obliques

15.2 Maintaining a proper form is crucial to exercising, especially when working the abs. Be sure to focus on the muscle you are working on. Visualise it tightening and releasing. It is better to do 12 properly formed crunches than 20 improperly formed crunches.

15.3 Stop immediately if you feel pain or discomfort in your back. It may be necessary to consult a trainer or your doctor to help you find a workout program that is right for you. Don't over strain yourself.

15.4 Do some form of aerobic exercise for 20 to 30 minutes at least thrice a week. There is no such thing as spot reducing. If you want to see the results of all that muscle work, you must remove the fat on top. Muscle work along will not achieve this.

15.5 A good diet is necessary. A high fat diet will negate all your efforts. Similarly, a starvation diet will also keep you from your goal. A balanced diet with protein, carbohydrates and fat is necessary to promote muscle gain and weight loss.

16

ROOTS OF
RESPONSIBILITY

The more conscious we are, we realise that our unconscious self is controlling our lives and thus not optimising our potential.

One of the techniques in spiritual living is to be conscious of one's feet whatever you do, let a part of your being be conscious of your feet. By his you give a "conscious shock" to your unconscious pattern. To give a conscious pause, conscious shock and conscious direction are steps towards enlightenment.

In between your busy schedule, give a 'conscious pause' and ask– are your thoughts mechanically happening or are you conscious? You find the answer as – it is mechanical. Now give a "conscious shock" and "consciously direct" yourself by being aware of your feet. By doing this you change yourself from being "head oriented". You descend to your feet.

When you are seated, feel your feet and imagine deep roots emerging from your feet and going deep into the earth. Feel these roots spreading and feel centred. Feel these roots are roots of goodness. Your basic responsibility is being a good individual. Generally we operate from whatever is "mine" is good, but extra-ordinary living comes from a paradigm where– whatever is "good" can be mine. Also imagine your roots are in devotion, in truth. Feel you are centred not only in goodness but in devotion and in truth. By practicing this you give a "conscious direction" to your life. The art of being spiritual is being centred. So practice it with devotion.

16.1 DO-ABLES

16.1.1 Always give a "conscious pause" then "conscious shock" and "conscious direction".

16.1.2 Be conscious of your feet

always.

16.1.3   While seated, feel the feet have roots and these are descending deep in the earth.

16.1.4   The roots are anchored in goodness, truth and devotion. Full yourself with this feeling.

17

BREATH RIGHT
TO BEAT FATIGUE

17.1 Proper breathing is essential for proper relaxation. The correct way to breathe is when you inhale, bring the abdomen out, and when you breathe out, take the abdomen in. The process should be as slow as it can be. Always try to follow this pattern in daily life.

17.2 Deep breathing technique Bhastrika helps in inhaling more oxygen, which helps energize the brain cells.

17.2.1 Go out in the open air.

17.2.2 Inhale and exhale rapidly through the nose for a minute. Do not retain the breath.

17.2.3 Relax for few seconds and repeat around 7-8 times at a stretch; but practice on an empty stomach.

17.3 YOGIC MASSAGE

Massage your ears and region around the ears using almond oil. This will release stress within a few seconds. It helps bring nutrients and oxygen to rejuvenate the brain cells.

17.4 LAUGHTER THERAPY

All of you should laugh at least three times a day. Laughter is key to god health and frees one from tension and worries. With laughter, our body, mind, brain, and entire nervous system reaches a perfect natural situation and deficiencies, as also ailments, are removed.

17.5 MUDRA

Practice of Pran Mudra and Apan Mudra helps reduce body fatigue.

Join the tips of ring finger and middle finger with the tip of the thumb, this forms the Apan Mudra with the practise of Apan Mudra, the body slowly gets purified. Join the tips of the ring and little fingers with that of the thumb, to form the Pran Mudra. Practice of this mudra rejuvenates the body.

18

HEALTH TIPS

18.1 Yoga or 45 minutes thrice a week helps a lot.

18.2 Try to eat satvik food (more fresh vegetables and fruits.) Avoid tea and coffee. Add more fibrous food to your diet. Drink at least three and half litres of water daily.

18.3 Try to control constipation with Isabgol, Trifala or Bel.

18.4 Drink lukewarm water.

18.5 Fast once a week.

18.6 Maintain regular sleep patterns.